CATHOLIC
ALL
JUNE

Catholic All June

Traditional Catholic prayers,
Bible passages, songs, and
devotions for the month of
the Sacred Heart

A COMPANION TO
THE CATHOLIC ALL YEAR COMPENDIUM

Kendra Tierney

/AINTE MARGUERITE·MARIE

ISBN: 9781098866785

ALSO BY KENDRA TIERNEY:

Catholic All January Prayer Booklet
Catholic All February Prayer Booklet
Catholic All March Prayer Booklet
Catholic All April Prayer Booklet
Catholic All May Booklet
Catholic All June Booklet
Catholic All Year Stations of the Cross Booklet
Catholic All Year A Visit to the Blessed
Sacrament Booklet
the above are available as printable pdfs at
www.CatholicAllYear.com or as paperback
booklets at www.Amazon.com

Catholic All Year Printable Lent featuring a
Lent Countdown Calendar, Voluntary Lenten
Discipline commitment slips, and a Lenten
Sacrifice Bean Jar label

Blessing of a Bonfire Booklet
May Crowning Booklet
Divine Mercy Novena Booklet
13 Month Liturgical Year Wall Calendar
Advent Wreath Prayers Booklet
Christmas Novena Booklet
At Home Nativity Play Booklet
Blessings for Candles and Throats Booklet
A Little Book About Confession for Children
My Superhero Prayer Book
My Fairy-Tale Prayer Book
My Woodland Prayer Book
The Catholic All Year Compendium

find them all at www.CatholicAllYear.com

Coming Soon: Prayers and Devotions Booklets
for July through December

User guide

Don't stress and don't think you have to do it all!

In this booklet, you'll find all the Bible passages, prayers, songs, and devotions for this month that our family uses to enhance our family prayer life and our liturgical living in the home. These are the prayers and practices that I recommend in my book, *The Catholic All Year Compendium*. There wasn't room in what was already a very long book to include all of them in the text, and they're all available right there on our phones.

Still, I don't know about you, but I really prefer paper over screens when I'm praying. I could blame it on the distractibility of my kids, but . . . I'm also pretty distractible. So, my plan is to create twelve of these booklets, one for each month. I'll keep them close at hand, for easy, screen-free access to the prayers, etc. that we like to use on various feast days. For all the history, tradition, and backstories surrounding these devotions and the feast days to which they are attached, please consult the book.

We try to work these prayers into our days in a way that doesn't add to our stress and busyness. We add a short prayer to the end of our grace before meals for the month, to help us stay mindful of the recommended devotion, and we add special litanies, prayers, and songs to our evening prayers as often as we are able, always depending on the circumstances of the day, week, year.

Many of these prayers are associated with indulgences, either partial or plenary (full), pursuant to the usual conditions. The Collect Prayers included come from that feast day's Mass propers, and a partial indulgence is available for the use of those prayers. See Appendix B of *The Catholic All Year Compendium* for a thorough explanation of indulgences.

℣ and ℟ in the text refer to "versicle" which is the leader's part, and "response" for everyone else.

Family 3 Special Days this month

BIRTHDAYS, NAMEDAYS, BAPTISM ANNIVERSARIES

_____

_____

_____

_____

_____

_____

_____

_____

_____

Table of Contents

Dear Reader,

The month of June is devoted to the Most Sacred
Heart of Jesus, and it's just chock full of opportunities
for plenary indulgences (and partial ones too)! Indulged
prayers and practices in this month's booklet include
the Consecration of the Family to the Sacred Heart
(which can be done any time), the Act of Reparation to
the Sacred Heart (to be said on the feast of the Sacred
Heart), two different plenary indulgences from which to
choose for the Solemnity of Saints Peter and Paul, and
a whole slew of partially indulged prayers, including
many litanies which are kid favorites in my house. A
partial indulgence is also attached to the included
collect prayer of each feast day. (Of course, a visit to
the Blessed Sacrament or a family Rosary are daily
opportunities to gain a plenary indulgence.)

There is a whole appendix on the whys and hows of
indulgences in the Compendium, and for ALL the info,
consult the Manual of Indulgences, but as a quick
refresher: "usual conditions" include intending to get
the indulgence, being baptized, being in a state of
grace, making a good confession (+/- twenty days),
receiving communion (+/- three days), reverently
following the instructions of the particular indulgence,
and praying for the Holy Father, the Pope (for example
an Our Father, Hail Mary, and Glory Be). One
confession can count for multiple indulgences,
everything else must be done for each indulgence
sought. Only one plenary indulgence can be gained per
day, unless one is in danger of death. Multiple partial

indulgences can be gained per day. If one cannot fulfill all the conditions of a plenary indulgence, it automatically becomes partial. Indulgences can be applied to oneself or to the soul of someone who has died, but not another living person. A "public recitation" is understood to be one which takes place in a church or oratory, or in a family, a religious community, or an association of the faithful, and in general when several of the faithful gather for some honest purpose.

Indulgences really are the ULTIMATE act of Christian charity, and are a beautiful thing of which to be mindful throughout the month of June and the whole liturgical year!

We have reached the end of the moveable feasts for the liturgical year with this booklet. Included here are Corpus Christi (a.k.a. the Feast of the Most Holy Body and Blood of Jesus) which falls the Second Sunday after Pentecost, and the feasts of the Sacred and Immaculate Hearts. Pentecost itself will sometimes fall in June, but more often it falls in May, so it's in the May booklet. Consult the moveable feasts page for the exact dates of moveable feasts.

Happy Summer (a.k.a. liturgical bonfire season),

Kendra Tierney

Kendra Tierney, 2019

Consecration
of the Family
TO THE SACRED HEART OF JESUS

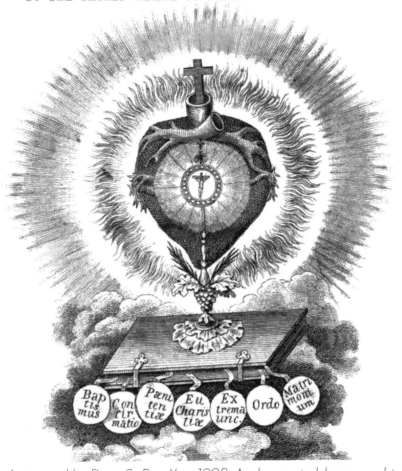

Approved by Pope St. Pius X in 1908. A plenary indulgence, subject to the usual conditions, is granted to the members of the family on the day on which it is first consecrated, if at all possible by a priest or deacon, to the Most Sacred Heart of Jesus, if they devoutly recite the duly approved prayer before an image of the Sacred Heart. On the anniversary of the consecration, a partial indulgence is available.
-Manual of Indulgences Grant 1

O Sacred Heart of Jesus, who made known to St. Margaret Mary your ardent desire to reign over Christian families, behold us assembled here today to proclaim your absolute dominion over our home.

Henceforth we purpose to lead a life like unto yours, so that among us may flourish the virtues for which you promised peace on earth, and for this end we will banish from our midst the spirit of the world which you abhor so much.

You will reign over our understanding by the simplicity of our faith. You will reign over our hearts by an ardent love for you; and may the flame of this love be ever kept burning in our hearts by the frequent reception of the Holy Eucharist.

Deign, O Divine Heart, to preside over our meetings, to bless our undertakings, both spiritual and temporal, to banish all worry and care, to sanctify our joys, and soothe our sorrows. If any of us should ever have the misfortune to grieve your Sacred Heart, remind him of your goodness and mercy towards the repentant sinner.

Lastly, when the hour of separation will sound, and death will plunge our home into mourning, then shall we all, and every one of us, be resigned to your eternal decrees, and seek consolation in the thought that we shall one day be reunited in Heaven, where we shall sing the praises and blessings of your Sacred Heart for all eternity.

May the Immaculate Heart of Mary, and the glorious Patriarch St. Joseph, offer you this our Consecration, and remind us of the same all the days of our life. Glory to the Divine Heart of Jesus, our King and our Father. Amen.

June: dedicated to the Sacred Heart

GRACE BEFORE MEALS:
Bless us, O Lord, and these thy gifts, which we are about to receive, from thy bounty, through Christ, Our Lord, Amen.

O SACRED HEART: *(From the Little Office of the Sacred Heart)*
O sacred Heart of Jesus, most obedient to the will of the Father, incline our hearts to you, that we may always do what is most pleasing to him. Amen.

Corpus Christi

THE MOST HOLY BODY AND BLOOD OF CHRIST
SECOND SUNDAY AFTER PENTECOST SOLEMNITY

COLLECT PRAYER

O God, who in this wonderful Sacrament have left us a memorial of your Passion, grant us, we pray, so to revere the sacred mysteries of your Body and Blood that we may always experience in ourselves the fruits of your redemption. Who live and reign with God the Father in the unity of the Holy Spirit, one God, for ever and ever. Amen.

BIBLE READING FOR THE FEAST John 6:52-59

The Jews quarreled among themselves, saying, "How can this man give us his flesh to eat?" Jesus said to them, "Amen, amen, I say to you, unless you eat the flesh of the Son of Man and drink his blood, you do not have life within you. Whoever eats my flesh and drinks my blood has eternal life, and I will raise him on the last day. For my flesh is true food, and my blood is true drink. Whoever eats my flesh and drinks my blood remains in me and I in him. Just as the living Father sent me and I have life because of the Father, so also the one who feeds on me will have life because of me. This is the bread that came down from heaven. Unlike your ancestors who ate and still died, whoever eats this bread will live forever." These things he said while teaching in the synagogue in Capernaum.

Prayers in Honor of the Blessed Sacrament

ACT OF SPIRITUAL COMMUNION

Useful when one is unable to attend daily Mass, at Mass but not in a state of grace or otherwise unable to receive Communion, or passing a Catholic church, but unable to stop in for visit to the Blessed Sacrament. A partial indulgence is available for the use of an approved prayer as an act of spiritual communion.

My Jesus, I believe that you are present in the Most Holy Sacrament. I love you above all things, and I desire to receive you into my soul.

Since I cannot at this moment receive you sacramentally, come at least spiritually into my heart. I embrace you as if you were already there and unite myself wholly to you. Never permit me to be separated from you. Amen.

or this one, which also works as a prayer of preparation before Communion . . .

I wish, Lord, to receive you with the purity, humility, and devotion with which your most holy Mother received you, with the spirit and fervour of the saints. Amen.

Prayers of thanksgiving after Communion

A partial indulgence is offered for making an act of thanksgiving after Communion using one of these two prayers.

ANIMA CHRISTI

Soul of Christ, sanctify me.
Body of Christ, save me.
Blood of Christ. inebriate me.
Water from the side of Christ, wash me.

Passion of Christ, strengthen me.
O Good Jesus, hear me.
Within your wounds hide me.
Permit me not to be separated from you.
From the wicked foe, defend me.
At the hour of my death, call me
and bid me come to you
That with your saints I may praise you
For ever and ever. Amen.

EN EGO, O BONE ET DULCISSIME IESU

Look down upon me, good and gentle Jesus, while before your face I humbly kneel, and with burning soul pray and beseech you to fix deep in my heart lively sentiments of faith, hope and charity, true contrition for my sins, and a firm purpose of amendment, while I contemplate with great love and tender pity your five wounds, pondering over them within me, calling to mind the words which David, your prophet, said of you, my good Jesus: "They have pierced my hands and my feet; they have numbered all my bones" *(Ps 21, 17-18)*.

Litany of the Most Precious Blood

This Litany in honor of Jesus in His Most Precious Blood was drawn up by the Sacred Congregation of Rites and promulgated by Pope John XXIII on February 24, 1960. A partial Indulgence is granted to the faithful who recite this litany.

℣

Lord, have mercy.
Christ, have mercy.
Lord, have mercy.
Jesus, hear us.

℟

Lord, have mercy.
Christ, have mercy.
Lord, have mercy.
Jesus, graciously hear us.

God our Father in heaven — Have mercy on us.
God, the Son, Redeemer of the world, — Have mercy on us.
God, the Holy Spirit, — Have mercy on us.
Holy Trinity, One God, — Have mercy on us.

Blood of Christ, only Son of the Father, — Be our salvation.
Blood of Christ, incarnate Word, — Be our salvation.
Blood of Christ, of the new and eternal covenant, — Be our salvation.
Blood of Christ, that spilled to the ground, — Be our salvation.
Blood of Christ, that flowed at the scourging, — Be our salvation.
Blood of Christ, dripping from the thorns, — Be our salvation.
Blood of Christ, shed on the cross, — Be our salvation.
Blood of Christ, the price of our redemption, — Be our salvation.
Blood of Christ, our only claim to pardon, — Be our salvation.
Blood of Christ, our blessing cup, — Be our salvation.
Blood of Christ, in which we are washed, — Be our salvation.
Blood of Christ, torrent of mercy, — Be our salvation.
Blood of Christ, that overcomes evil, — Be our salvation.
Blood of Christ, strength of the martyrs, — Be our salvation.

continued

℣	℟

Blood of Christ, endurance of the
saints,   Be our salvation.
Blood of Christ, that makes the
barren fruitful,   Be our salvation.
Blood of Christ, protection of the
threatened,   Be our salvation.
Blood of Christ, comfort of the weary. Be our salvation.
Blood of Christ, solace of the mourner, Be our salvation.
Blood of Christ, hope of the repentant, Be our salvation.
Blood of Christ, consolation of the
dying,   Be our salvation.
Blood of Christ, our peace and
refreshment,   Be our salvation.
Blood of Christ, our pledge of life,   Be our salvation.
Blood of Christ, by which we pass to
glory,   Be our salvation.
Blood of Christ, most worthy of honor, Be our salvation.

Lamb of God, who takes away the
sins of the world,   Have mercy on us.
Lamb of God, who takes away the
sins of the world,   Have mercy on us.
Lamb of God, who takes away the
sins of the world,   Have mercy on us.

Lord, you redeemed us by your blood,   You have made
us a kingdom to
Let us pray.   serve our God.

Father, by the blood of your Son you have set us free
and saved us from death. Continue your work of love
within us, that by constantly celebrating the mystery of
our salvation we may reach the eternal life it promises.
We ask this through Christ our Lord.

     Amen.

Sacred Heart

COLLECT PRAYER
Grant, we pray, almighty God, that we, who glory in the
Heart of your beloved Son and recall the wonders of his
love for us, may be made worthy to receive an
overflowing measure of grace from that fount of
heavenly gifts. Through our Lord Jesus Christ, your
Son, who lives and reigns with you in the unity of the
Holy Spirit, one God, for ever and ever. Amen.

Act of Reparation

TO THE SACRED HEART OF JESUS

A plenary indulgence is granted, subject to the usual conditions, to the the faithful who, on the solemnity of the Most Sacred Heart of Jesus, publicly recite the act of reparation. A partial indulgence is granted for its use in other circumstances.

Most sweet Jesus, you have bestowed on men the benefits of your charity, but their ingratitude only responds with forgetfulness, negligence and spite. Thus here we prostrate ourselves before your altar, inspired by the desire to make reparation through a special homage for their culpable indifference and the outrages which, in all ways, they oppress your most loving Heart.

Nevertheless, we remember that we ourselves have been guilty of unworthy conduct in the past, and filled with profound sorrow, we implore your mercy for us first of all. By voluntary expiation, we are ready to atone for the faults we have committed, ready also to expiate for those who, led astray from the way of salvation and remaining obstinate in their infidelity, refuse to follow you, their Shepherd and chief, thus throwing off the yoke of your law and trampling the promises of their Baptism.

We would like to expiate for too many lamentable faults, making reparation for each of the following: our disorderly conduct, indecent fashions, scandalous corruption of innocent souls, profanation of Sundays and feasts, detestable blasphemies against you and against your saints, insults to your vicar and to your priests, reckless violations and odious sacrileges to the divine Sacrament of your love, and finally the public sins of nations who revolt against the rights and authority of your Church.

continued

If only we could erase so many offenses with our own blood! At the least we wish to make reparation to your outraged honor. We present to you even the satisfaction that you have offered to your Father on the Cross, and the offering you have renewed each day on the altar. We present that sacrifice to you, accompanied with all the acts of atonement made by the Most Holy Virgin your Mother, the Saints, and by faithful Christians. We promise you with all of our hearts, with the help of your grace, to use all our means to do penance for our past faults and those of our neighbor. By the fervor of our faith, the purity of our life, and by perfect docility to the precepts of the Gospel, we desire to atone for the indifference toward such a great love, to which belongs all charity. We also promise you to make every effort to spare you new offenses and to lead the most souls possible to follow you.

Agreed, we offer you in this matter, O most good Jesus, by the intercession of the gracious Virgin Mary, Reparatrix, this spontaneous homage of expiation. Guard us until death, keeping us unshakably faithful to our duty and to your service. Accord to us this precious gift of perseverance, which leads us finally to our native land where, with the Father and the Holy Spirit, You reign, God, forever and ever. Amen.

MORNING OFFERING *This prayer, which invokes the Sacred and Immaculate Hearts, is perfect for these feast days, but is also an excellent way to begin EVERY day.*

O my Jesus, through the Immaculate Heart of Mary, I offer you all my prayers, works, joys, and sufferings of this day, for all the intentions of your Sacred Heart, in union with the Holy Sacrifice of the Mass offered throughout the world, in reparation for my sins, for the intentions of all my relatives and friends, and in particular for the intentions of the Holy Father. Amen.

Litany of the Sacred Heart of Jesus

Based on litanies that date back to the 17th century, this version has 33 invocations, one for each year Jesus' life, and was approved for public use by Pope Leo XIII in 1899.

℣	℟
Lord, have mercy.	Lord, have mercy.
Christ, have mercy.	Christ, have mercy.
Lord, have mercy.	Lord, have mercy.
Jesus, hear us.	Jesus, graciously hear us.

God our Father in heaven, — Have mercy on us.
God, the Son, Redeemer of the world, — Have mercy on us.
God, the Holy Spirit, — Have mercy on us.
Holy Trinity, One God, — Have mercy on us.

Heart of Jesus, Son of the Eternal Father, — Have mercy on us.
Heart of Jesus, formed by the Holy Spirit in the womb of the Virgin Mother, — Have mercy on us.
Heart of Jesus, substantially united to the Word of God, — Have mercy on us.
Heart of Jesus, of Infinite Majesty, — Have mercy on us.
Heart of Jesus, Sacred Temple of God, — Have mercy on us.
Heart of Jesus, Tabernacle of the Most High, — Have mercy on us.
Heart of Jesus, House of God and Gate of Heaven, — Have mercy on us.
Heart of Jesus, burning furnace of charity, — Have mercy on us.
Heart of Jesus, abode of justice and love, — Have mercy on us.
Heart of Jesus, full of goodness and love, — Have mercy on us.
Heart of Jesus, abyss of all virtues, — Have mercy on us.

continued

℣ ℟

Heart of Jesus, most worthy of all praise,	Have mercy on us.
Heart of Jesus, king and center of all hearts,	Have mercy on us.
Heart of Jesus, in whom are all treasures of wisdom and knowledge,	Have mercy on us.
Heart of Jesus, in whom dwells the fullness of divinity,	Have mercy on us.
Heart of Jesus, in whom the Father was well pleased,	Have mercy on us.
Heart of Jesus, of whose fullness we have all received,	Have mercy on us.
Heart of Jesus, desire of the everlasting hills,	Have mercy on us.
Heart of Jesus, patient and most merciful,	Have mercy on us.
Heart of Jesus, enriching all who invoke you,	Have mercy on us.
Heart of Jesus, fountain of life and holiness,	Have mercy on us.
Heart of Jesus, propitiation for our sins,	Have mercy on us.
Heart of Jesus, loaded down with opprobrium,	Have mercy on us.
Heart of Jesus, bruised for our offenses,	Have mercy on us.
Heart of Jesus, obedient to death,	Have mercy on us.
Heart of Jesus, pierced with a lance,	Have mercy on us.
Heart of Jesus, source of all consolation,	Have mercy on us.
Heart of Jesus, our life and resurrection,	Have mercy on us.
Heart of Jesus, our peace and our reconciliation,	Have mercy on us.
Heart of Jesus, victim for our sins,	Have mercy on us.
Heart of Jesus, salvation of those who trust in you,	Have mercy on us.
Heart of Jesus, hope of those who die in you,	Have mercy on us.
Heart of Jesus, delight of all the Saints,	Have mercy on us.

continued

V̇	Ṙ

Lamb of God, who takes away
   the sins of the world,   Spare us, O Lord.
Lamb of God, who takes away
   the sins of the world,   Graciously hear us, O Lord.
Lamb of God, who takes away
   the sins of the world.   Have mercy on us

Jesus, meek and humble of
   heart.   Make our hearts like to
                                   thine.
Let us pray.
Almighty and eternal God, look upon the Heart of your
most beloved Son and upon the praises and
satisfaction which he offers you in the name of sinners;
and to those who implore your mercy, in your great
goodness, grant forgiveness in the name of the same
Jesus Christ, your Son, who lives and reigns with you
forever and ever.   Amen.

PRAYER TO THE SACRED HEART FOR HELP TO FORGIVE

Lord Jesus, my heart feels like an impenetrable stone
as I am struggling to forgive _____.
Please trade my hardened heart for one that flows with
mercy like your own.
Give me the grace to let go of bitterness, a desire for
revenge, and the need for an apology.
Set me free from the captivity of my unforgiving heart
and fill me with your healing love. Amen.

Immaculate Heart

of the Blessed Virgin Mary

SATURDAY AFTER CORPUS CHRISTI MEMORIAL

COLLECT PRAYER

Grant, Lord God, that we, your servants, may rejoice in unfailing health of mind and body, and, through the glorious intercession of Blessed Mary ever-Virgin, may we be set free from present sorrow and come to enjoy eternal happiness. Amen.

PRAYER TO THE IMMACULATE HEART OF MARY

Immaculate Heart of Mary,
full of love for God and mankind,
and of compassion for sinners,
I consecrate myself to you.
I entrust to you the salvation of my soul.

May my heart be ever united with yours,
so that I may hate sin,
love God and my neighbor,
and reach eternal life with those whom I love.

May I experience the kindness of your motherly heart
and the power of your intercession with Jesus
during my life and at the hour of my death.
Amen.

Litany of Loreto

The Litany of the Blessed Virgin Mary is a Marian litany approved in 1587 by Pope Sixtus V. The litany is usually recited as a call and response in a group setting. A partial indulgence is attached to the prayer at any time. We recite The Litany of Loreto on all Marian feast days.

℣

℟

Lord, have mercy on us.
Lord, have mercy on us.
Christ, hear us.

Christ, have mercy on us.
Christ, have mercy on us.
Christ, graciously hear us.

God the Father of Heaven,
God the Son, Redeemer of the world,
God the Holy Spirit,
Holy Trinity, One God,

Have mercy on us.
Have mercy on us.
Have mercy on us.
Have mercy on us.

Holy Mary,
Holy Mother of God,
Holy Virgin of virgins,
Mother of Christ,
Mother of the Church,
Mother of divine grace,
Mother most pure,
Mother most chaste,
Mother inviolate,
Mother undefiled,
Mother most amiable,
Mother most admirable,
Mother of good counsel,
Mother of our Creator,
Mother of our Savior,
Virgin most prudent,
Virgin most venerable,
Virgin most renowned,
Virgin most powerful,
Virgin most merciful,
Virgin most faithful,
Mirror of justice,
Seat of wisdom,
Cause of our joy,
Spiritual vessel,

Pray for us.
Pray for us.
Pray for us.
Pray for us.
Pray for us.
Pray for us.
Pray for us.
Pray for us.
Pray for us.
Pray for us.
Pray for us.
Pray for us.
Pray for us.
Pray for us.
Pray for us.
Pray for us.
Pray for us.
Pray for us.
Pray for us.
Pray for us.
Pray for us.
Pray for us.
Pray for us.
Pray for us.
Pray for us.

continued

℣		℟
Vessel of honor,		Pray for us.
Singular vessel of devotion,		Pray for us.
Mystical rose,		Pray for us.
Tower of David,		Pray for us.
Tower of ivory,		Pray for us.
House of gold,		Pray for us.
Ark of the covenant,		Pray for us.
Gate of Heaven,		Pray for us.
Morning star,		Pray for us.
Health of the sick,		Pray for us.
Refuge of sinners,		Pray for us.
Comforter of the afflicted,		Pray for us.
Help of Christians,		Pray for us.
Queen of angels,		Pray for us.
Queen of patriarchs,		Pray for us.
Queen of prophets,		Pray for us.
Queen of apostles,		Pray for us.
Queen of martyrs,		Pray for us.
Queen of confessors,		Pray for us.
Queen of virgins,		Pray for us.
Queen of all saints,		Pray for us.
Queen conceived without Original Sin,		Pray for us.
Queen assumed into Heaven,		Pray for us.
Queen of the holy Rosary,		Pray for us.
Queen of families,		Pray for us.
Queen of peace,		Pray for us.

Lamb of God, who takes away
the sins of the world,   Spare us, O Lord.
Lamb of God, who takes away
the sins of the world,   Graciously spare us, O Lord.
Lamb of God, who takes away
the sins of the world,   Have mercy on us.

Pray for us, O holy Mother of   That we may be made
God,   worthy of the
                                                      promises of Christ.
Let us pray.
Grant, we beseech thee, O Lord God, that we, your
servants, may enjoy perpetual health of mind and
body; and by the intercession of the Blessed Mary, ever
Virgin, may be delivered from present sorrow, and
obtain eternal joy. Through Christ our Lord.   Amen.

Saint Anthony

COLLECT PRAYER

Almighty ever-living God, who gave Saint Anthony of
Padua to your people as an outstanding preacher and
an intercessor in their need, grant that, with his
assistance, as we follow the teachings of the Christian
life, we may know your help in every trial. Through our
Lord Jesus Christ, your Son, who lives and reigns with
you in the unity of the Holy Spirit, one God, for ever
and ever. Amen.

SI QUAERIS

*This prayer of praise in honor of Saint Anthony was composed by
friar Julian of Speyer. It is part of the Officium rhythmicum S. Antonii,
which dates back to 1233, two years after Saint Anthony's death. It is
sung at Saint Anthony's Basilica and many other churches every
Tuesday.*

If then you ask for miracles,
death, error, all calamities,
leprosy and demons fly,
and health succeeds
infirmities.
The sea obeys and
fetters break,
and lifeless limbs you
do restore;
while treasures lost are found
again,
men young and old your aid
implore.

All dangers vanish at your prayer,
and direst need does quickly flee;
Let those who know your power
proclaim,
Let Paduans say: these are yours.
To Father, Son may glory be
And Holy Spirit, eternally.
Amen.

Saint Josemaria Novena of Work

Written by Francisco Faus, this novena includes quotes from St. Josemaría's writings, and is appropriate to pray for the sanctification of work in and out of the home, or when seeking a job. It can be begun on June 17th, to end on the vigil of the feast of St. Josemaría, or prayed any time.

INTRO PRAYER *start each day's novena with this prayer*
O God, through the intercession of the Most Blessed Virgin Mary, you granted countless graces to your priest St. Josemaria, choosing him as a most faithful instrument to found Opus Dei, a way to holiness through daily work and the ordinary duties of a Christian.

Grant that I also may learn to turn all the circumstances and events of my life into opportunities to love you and serve the Church, the Pope, and all souls, with joy and simplicity, lighting up the paths of the earth with faith and love.

Through the intercession of St. Josemaria, please grant me the favor I request *(mention your request here)*. Amen.

CONCLUDING PRAYER *end each day's novena with these prayers*
Our Father, Hail Mary, Glory Be.

continued

DAY 1: *"We have come to call attention once again to the example of Jesus, who spent thirty years in Nazareth, working as a carpenter. In his hands, a professional occupation, similar to that carried out by millions of people all over the world, was turned into a divine task. It became a part of our Redemption, a way to salvation."* (Conversations with Monsignor Josemaría Escrivá, 55)

May our Lord God help me see my work as a path to holiness and a service to others, where God my Father awaits me at every moment, asking me, in each situation, to imitate Jesus when he worked as a carpenter in Nazareth.

DAY 2: *"The dignity of work is founded on Love. Man's great privilege is to be able to love, transcending from what is fleeting and ephemeral."* (Christ is Passing By, 48)

May our Lord God help me to understand that what gives value to any honest work is the love with which I do it: love for God, in the first place, to whom I can offer up my work; and love for my neighbour, whom I wish to serve and be useful to.

DAY 3: *"How short indeed is the time of our passing through this world! For the true Christian these words ring deep down in his heart as a reproach to his lack of generosity, and as a constant invitation to be loyal. Brief indeed is our time for loving, for giving, for making atonement. It would be very wrong, therefore, for us to waste it, or to cast this treasure irresponsibly overboard. We mustn't squander this period of the world's history that God has entrusted to each one of us."* (Friends of God, 39)

With the help of the Most Blessed Virgin Mary, may I learn to use my time as the treasure it is, and make the effort to improve in the virtue of order, so as to work more punctually, intensely and constantly, without disorder or delays. May I achieve this by following a well-structured plan, which allows for me to spend the appropriate amount of time on each of my duties: spiritual life, family life, professional life, and social relations, in a balanced way.

continued

DAY 4: *"It is no good offering to God something that is less perfect than our poor human limitations permit. The work that we offer must be without blemish and it must be done as carefully as possible, even in its smallest details, for God will not accept shoddy workmanship. 'Thou shalt not offer anything that is faulty,' Holy Scripture warns us (Lev 22:20), 'because it would not be worthy of him.'*

For that reason, the work of each one of us, the activities that take up our time and energy, must be an offering worthy of our Creator. It must be operatio Dei, a work of God that is done for God: in short, a task that is complete and faultless." (Friends of God, 55)

May God help me to work well, with the greatest possible perfection. May I never work carelessly, but be convinced that work done badly cannot be sanctified, because it lacks love, and love alone enables any human action to be pleasing to God.

DAY 5: *"It is time for us Christians to shout from the rooftops that work is a gift from God and that it makes no sense to classify men differently, according to their occupation, as if some jobs were nobler than others. Work, all work, bears witness to the dignity of man, to his dominion over creation."* (Christ is Passing By, 47)

If my present job is below my level of competence and my legitimate aspirations, may I not belittle it. Rather, while seeking something more appropriate, may I carry it out in a fully responsible way, giving it the same value as Jesus gave his work at Nazareth.

DAY 6: *"I beg you, don't ever lose the supernatural point of view. Correct your intention as the course of a ship is corrected on the high seas: by looking at the star, by looking at Mary. Then you will always be sure of reaching harbour."* (The Forge, 749)

May God open the eyes of my soul to understand that he is always at my side. So as not to lose sight of this marvelous reality, may I make the effort to stay in God's presence during my work, using as a discreet reminder a small crucifix, or a small picture of Our

continued

Lady or of some saint to whom I have devotion, positioned where I can see it often, without attracting unnecessary attention.

DAY 7: *"Everything in which we poor human beings intervene—even sanctity—is a tissue of small trifles, which—depending on the purity of our intention—can form a tapestry of splendid heroism or of meanness, of virtues or of sins."* (The Way, 826)

May God help me to develop the Christian virtues and to mature spiritually through the work I do. May I seek to be patient and understanding, both towards my managers and towards my colleagues and subordinates. May I be simple and humble, avoiding vanity and exhibitionism. In a word, may I do everything with purity of heart.

DAY 8: *"Consider too that, by doing your daily work well and responsibly, not only will you be supporting yourselves financially, you will also be contributing in a very direct way to the development of society, you will be relieving the burdens of others and maintaining countless welfare projects, both local and international, on behalf of less privileged individuals and countries."* (Friends of God, 120)

May God infuse in my soul the desire to make of my work, not a self-centered activity geared to my own interests, but a service that is open and useful to many, done in the certainty that this ideal of service to others will give a new, higher and more joyful meaning to my life.

DAY 9: *"Professional work is also apostolate, an opportunity to give ourselves to others, to reveal Christ to them and lead them to God the Father."* (Christ is Passing By, 49)

May God help me see in the area of my work, a wide field for the apostolic mission that God entrusts to all the baptized, using the opportunities he offers me to help my colleagues, friends, and clients discover the marvels of the Christian faith.

Saints John Fisher and Thomas More

COLLECT PRAYER

O God, who in martyrdom have brought true faith to its highest expression, graciously grant that, strengthened through the intercession of Saints John Fisher and Thomas More, we may confirm by the witness of our life the faith we profess with our lips. Through our Lord Jesus Christ, your Son, who lives and reigns with you in the unity of the Holy Spirit, one God, for ever and ever. Amen.

PRAYER FOR GOOD HUMOR by St. Thomas More

Grant me, O Lord, good digestion, and also something to digest.
Grant me a healthy body, and the necessary good humor to maintain it.
Grant me a simple soul that knows to treasure all that is good
and that doesn't frighten easily at the sight of evil,
but rather finds the means to put things back in their place.
Give me a soul that knows not boredom, grumblings, sighs and laments,
nor excess of stress, because of that obstructing thing called "I."
Grant me, O Lord, a sense of good humor.
Allow me the grace to be able to take a joke,
to discover in life a bit of joy,
and to be able to share it with others.
Amen.

Blessing of a Bonfire

One of the oldest blessings of the Catholic Church, it has been practiced on the Eve of the Nativity of St. John the Baptist (June 23rd) since ancient times. This version is adapted from the 1964 Roman Ritual. The Gregorian Chant hymn Ut queant laxis can be substituted for the two part Canticle of Zechariah.

OPENING PRAYER

℣: Our help is in the name of the Lord.
℞: Who made heaven and earth.

℣: The Lord be with you.
℞: May he also be with you.

BIBLE READING *Matthew 3:11*

I am baptizing you with water, for repentance, but the one who is coming after me is mightier than I. I am not worthy to carry his sandals. He will baptize you with the holy Spirit and fire.

BLESSING *The blessing is performed by a priest if possible, otherwise by the head of household, who recites the blessing and sprinkles the holy water but does not make any hand gestures.*

℣: Let us pray.
Lord God, almighty Father, the light that never fails and the source of all light, sanctify + this new fire, and grant that after the darkness of this life we may come unsullied to you who are light eternal; through Christ our Lord.
℞: Amen.

The fire is sprinkled with holy water.
℣: There was a man sent from God.
℞: Whose name was John.

continued

The Canticle of Zechariah

a.k.a. The Benedictus, based on Luke 1:68-79. Can be recited in two groups, or individually.

GROUP 1: Blessed be the Lord, the God of Israel; he has come to his people and set them free.

GROUP 2: He has raised up for us a mighty Saviour, born of the house of his servant David.

GROUP 1: Through his holy prophets he promised of old that he would save us from our enemies, from the hands of all who hate us.

GROUP 2: He promised to show mercy to our fathers and to remember his holy Covenant.

GROUP 1: This was the oath he swore to our father Abraham: to set us free from the hands of our enemies, free to worship him without fear, holy and righteous in his sight, all the days of our life.

GROUP 2: You, my child shall be called the prophet of the Most High, for you will go before the Lord to prepare his way, to give his people knowledge of salvation by the forgiveness of their sins.

GROUP 1: In the tender compassion of our Lord the dawn from on high shall break upon us, to shine on those who dwell in darkness

GROUP 2: And the shadow of death, and to guide our feet into the way of peace.

ALL: Glory to the Father, and to the Son, and to the Holy Spirit.
As it was in the beginning. is now, and will be forever.
Amen.

continued

CLOSING PRAYER

℣: Let us pray. God, who by reason of the birth of blessed John have made this day praiseworthy, give your people the grace of spiritual joy, and keep the hearts of your faithful fixed on the way that leads to everlasting salvation; through Christ our Lord.
℟: Amen

John the Baptist never sinned and was sanctified in his mother's womb. And I have committed so many sins . . .
—*Saint Catherine of Siena, A Treatise of Prayer, 1370.*

Nativity of Saint John the Baptist

COLLECT PRAYER

Grant, we pray, almighty God, that your family may walk in the way of salvation and, attentive to what Saint John the Precursor urged, may come safely to the One he foretold, our Lord Jesus Christ, who lives and reigns with you in the unity of the Holy Spirit, one God, for ever and ever. Amen.

BIBLE READING FOR THE FEAST *Luke 1:57-66, 80*

When the time arrived for Elizabeth to have her child she gave birth to a son. Her neighbors and relatives heard that the Lord had shown his great mercy toward her, and they rejoiced with her. When they came on the eighth day to circumcise the child, they were going to call him Zechariah after his father, but his mother said in reply, "No. He will be called John." But they answered her, "There is no one among your relatives who has this name." So they made signs, asking his father what he wished him to be called. He asked for a tablet and wrote, "John is his name," and all were amazed. Immediately his mouth was opened, his tongue freed, and he spoke blessing God. Then fear came upon all their neighbors, and all these matters were discussed throughout the hill country of Judea. All who heard these things took them to heart, saying, "What, then, will this child be?" For surely the hand of the Lord was with him.

The child grew and became strong in spirit, and he was in the desert until the day of his manifestation to Israel.

Litany of Saint John the Baptist

℣   ℟

Lord, have mercy.   Lord, have mercy.
Christ, have mercy.   Christ, have mercy.
Lord, have mercy.   Lord, have mercy.
Jesus, hear us.   Jesus, graciously hear us.

God, the Father of Heaven,   Have mercy on us.
God, the Son, Redeemer of the
    world,   Have mercy on us.
God, the Holy Spirit,   Have mercy on us.
Holy Trinity, One God,   Have mercy on us.

Holy Mary,   Pray for us.
Queen of Prophets,   Pray for us.
Queen of Martyrs,   Pray for us.

Saint John the Baptist,   Pray for us.
St. John the Baptist, precursor of Christ,   Pray for us.
St. John the Baptist, glorious forerunner
    of the Sun of Justice,   Pray for us.
St. John the Baptist, minister of
    baptism to Jesus,   Pray for us.
St. John the Baptist, burning and
    shining lamp of the world,   Pray for us.
St. John the Baptist, angel of purity
    before your birth,   Pray for us.
St. John the Baptist, special friend and
    favorite of Christ,   Pray for us.
St. John the Baptist, heavenly
    contemplative, whose element was
    prayer,   Pray for us.
St. John the Baptist, intrepid preacher
    of truth,   Pray for us.
St. John the Baptist, voice crying in the
    wilderness,   Pray for us.
St. John the Baptist, miracle of
    mortification and penance,   Pray for us.

continued

St. John the Baptist, example of profound humility,	Pray for us.
St. John the Baptist, glorious martyr of zeal for God's holy law,	Pray for us.
St. John the Baptist, gloriously fulfilling your mission,	Pray for us.

Lamb of God, who takes away the sins of the world,	Spare us, O Lord.
Lamb of God, who takes away the sins of the world,	Graciously hear us, O Lord.
Lamb of God, who takes away the sins of the world.	Have mercy on us

Pray for us, O glorious St. John the Baptist,   That we may be made worthy of the promises of Christ.

Let us pray,
O God, who have honored this world by the birth of Saint John the Baptist, grant that your faithful people may rejoice in the way of eternal salvation, through Jesus Christ Our Lord.

Amen.

Saint Josemaría Escrivá

COLLECT PRAYER

Grant, O Lord, that we may always revere and love
your holy name, for you never deprive of your guidance
those you set firm on the foundation of your love.
Through our Lord Jesus Christ, your Son, who lives and
reigns with you in the unity of the Holy Spirit, one God,
for ever and ever. Amen.

PRAYER OF ABANDONMENT TO GOD'S PROVIDENCE

by Saint Josemaría Escrivá

My Lord and my God:
into your hands I abandon the past and the present
and the future,
what is small and what is great,
what amounts to a little and what amounts to a lot,
things temporal and things eternal.
Amen.

Saints Peter and Paul

COLLECT PRAYER

Grant, we pray, O Lord our God, that we may be sustained by the intercession of the blessed Apostles Peter and Paul, that, as through them you gave your Church the foundations of her heavenly office, so through them you may help her to eternal salvation. Through our Lord Jesus Christ, your Son, who lives and reigns with you in the unity of the Holy Spirit, one God, for ever and ever. Amen.

BIBLE READING FOR THE FEAST *Galatians 2:7-14*

a.k.a. The Incident at Antioch

On the contrary, when they saw that I had been entrusted with the gospel to the uncircumcised, just as Peter to the circumcised, for the one who worked in Peter for an apostolate to the circumcised worked also in me for the Gentiles, and when they recognized the grace bestowed upon me, James and Cephas and John, who were reputed to be pillars, gave me and Barnabas their right hands in partnership, that we should go to the Gentiles and they to the circumcised. Only, we were to be mindful of the poor, which is the very thing I was eager to do.

And when Cephas came to Antioch, I opposed him to his face because he clearly was wrong. For, until some people came from James, he used to eat with the Gentiles; but when they came, he began to draw back and separated himself, because he was afraid of the circumcised. And the rest of the Jews also acted hypocritically along with him, with the result that even Barnabas was carried away by their hypocrisy. But when I saw that they were not on the right road in line with the truth of the gospel, I said to Cephas in front of all, "If you, though a Jew, are living like a Gentile and not like a Jew, how can you compel the Gentiles to live like Jews?"

Indulgences

HOLY APOSTLES PETER AND PAUL, INTERCEDE FOR US.

partial indulgence available for devout recitation any time

Guard your people, who rely on the patronage of your apostles Peter and Paul, O Lord, and keep them under your continual protection. Through Christ our Lord, Amen.

A plenary indulgence, subject to the usual conditions, is granted to the faithful who, on the Solemnity of the Holy Apostles Peter and Paul, make prayerful use of an article of devotion (a properly blessed crucifix or cross, rosary, scapular, or medal) that has been blessed by the Supreme Pontiff or by any bishop, provided the faithful also make a Profession of Faith using any legitimate formula (The Nicene Creed or the Apostles' Creed). A partial indulgence is granted to the faithful who devoutly use such articles of devotion properly blessed by either a priest or a deacon. - Manual of Indulgences, Grant 14

A different plenary indulgence is available on this feast day for making a pious visit—with the purpose of expressing during the visit filial submission to the pope—to one of the four Patriarchal Basilicas of Rome, or a local minor basilica, or the cathedral church of your diocese, and there reciting the Our Father and the Creed.
- Manual of Indulgences, Grant 33

The Nicene Creed

I believe in one God,
the Father almighty,
maker of heaven and earth,
of all things visible and invisible.

I believe in one Lord Jesus Christ,
the Only Begotten Son of God,
born of the Father before all ages.
God from God, Light from Light,
true God from true God,
begotten, not made, consubstantial with the Father;
through him all things were made.
For us men and for our salvation
he came down from heaven,
and by the Holy Spirit was incarnate of the Virgin
Mary,
and became man.
For our sake he was crucified under Pontius Pilate,
he suffered death and was buried,
and rose again on the third day
in accordance with the Scriptures.
He ascended into heaven
and is seated at the right hand of the Father.
He will come again in glory
to judge the living and the dead
and his kingdom will have no end.

I believe in the Holy Spirit, the Lord, the giver of life,
who proceeds from the Father and the Son,
who with the Father and the Son is adored and
glorified,
who has spoken through the prophets.

I believe in one, holy, catholic and apostolic Church.
I confess one Baptism for the forgiveness of sins
and I look forward to the resurrection of the dead
and the life of the world to come. Amen.

Moveable feasts

ASH WEDNESDAY
March 6, 2019
February 26, 2020
February 17, 2021
March 2, 2022
February 22, 2023
February 14, 2024
March 5, 2025
February 18, 2026
February 10, 2027
March 1, 2028
February 14, 2029

EASTER
April 21, 2019
April 12, 2020
April 4, 2021
April 17, 2022
April 9, 2023
March 31, 2024
April 20, 2025
April 5, 2026
March 28, 2027
April 16, 2028
April 1, 2029

ASCENSION (THURSDAY)
May 30, 2019
May 21, 2020
May 13, 2021
May 26, 2022
May 18, 2023
May 9, 2024
May 29, 2025
May 14, 2026
May 6, 2027
May 25, 2028
May 10, 2029

ASCENSION (SUNDAY)
June 2, 2019
May 24, 2020
May 16, 2021
May 29, 2022
May 21, 2023
May 12, 2024
June 1, 2025
May 17, 2026
May 9, 2027
May 28, 2028
May 13, 2029

PENTECOST
June 9, 2019
May 31, 2020
May 23, 2021
June 5, 2022
May 28, 2023
May 19, 2024
June 8, 2025
May 24, 2026
May 16, 2027
June 4, 2028
May 20, 2029

TRINITY SUNDAY
June 16, 2019
June 7, 2020
May 30, 2021
June 12, 2022
June 4, 2023
May 26, 2024
June 15, 2025
May 31, 2026
May 23, 2027
June 11, 2028
May 27, 2029

CORPUS CHRISTI (THURSDAY)
June 20, 2019
June 11, 2020
June 3, 2021
June 16, 2022
June 8, 2023
May 30, 2024
June 19, 2025
June 4, 2026
May 27, 2027
June 15, 2028
May 31, 2029

CORPUS CHRISTI (SUNDAY)
June 23, 2019
June 14, 2020
June 6, 2021
June 19, 2022
June 11, 2023
June 2, 2024
June 22, 2025
June 7, 2026
May 30, 2027
June 18, 2028
June 3, 2029

SACRED HEART (FRIDAY)
June 28, 2019
June 19, 2020
June 11, 2021
June 24, 2022
June 16, 2023
June 7, 2024
June 27, 2025
June 12, 2026
June 4, 2027
June 23, 2028
June 8, 2029

IMMACULATE HEART IS THE NEXT DAY (SATURDAY)

Made in the
USA
Middletown, DE